NIGHTSHADE

Also by Andrea Cohen

Unfathoming
Furs Not Mine
Kentucky Derby
Long Division
The Cartographer's Vacation

NIGHTSHADE

Andrea Cohen

Four Way Books
Tribeca

Library of Congress Cataloging-in-Publication Data

Names: Cohen, Andrea, 1961- author.
Title: Nightshade / Andrea Cohen.
Description: New York, NY : Four Way Books, [2019]
Identifiers: LCCN 2019004728 | ISBN 9781945588358 (paperback : alk. paper)
Classification: LCC PS3603.O3415 A6 2019 | DDC 811/.6--dc23
LC record available at https://lccn.loc.gov/2019004728

This book is manufactured in the United States of America and printed on
acid-free paper.

Four Way Books is a not-for-profit literary press. We are grateful for the assistance
we receive from individual donors, public arts agencies, and private foundations.

This publication is made possible with public funds from the
National Endowment for the Arts

and from the New York State Council on the Arts, a state agency.

We are a proud member of the Community of Literary Magazines and Presses.

for
my father

and for
Amy Anderson

I know what I have given you. I do not know what you have received.
  —Antonio Porchia

Contents

I

II

III

Major to Minor

Trains jump tracks,
and people from

steep trestles leap.
But mostly it's

the subtler shifts
that hit us hard:

the key to the city
not quite fitting, the

epiphany of twin
beds where there

was one—like two
icebergs no July

knows what
          to do with.

The Size of It

They made oceans
big so one boat

going would seem
small. The sail

of your dinghy
obliterates the sun—

they were wrong.

Division Of

You took the painting
of the girl on the stair.

You left the stair.
You took the nail

on which the girl
in a pink haze hung.

You left the hole
in horsehair plaster—

and the crumbling
that comes after.

Spell

When she left
we halved

everything
but absence.

I didn't buy
another bed,

but slept
on the floor.

It was good
for a spell

to have nothing
to fall out of.

Action Origami

How much can you do
with one piece of paper—
creasing, tearing, adding
volume with air? You can
make a mythic sea
monster toppling a tall
ship in high, high seas, as
my seatmate in 30C did
in sixteen hours. He was
from Saipan, an island
advertised as a pearl
arrived at by sea or air. This
should have been a six-
hour trip from Boston
to San Francisco, but mostly
we sat on the tarmac, iced
in, waiting, as I did in a similar
but different blizzard in '83,
on a People's Express flight
from Logan to JFK. I was going
to Park Ave to see a specialist in
what I had. We called it homosexuality
then, or my parents did, and my father
was convinced it was his fault, on
account of his queer cousin in Augusta,
and his schizophrenic brother. I was
going to the specialist for them, was

going to die in the plane crash
for them, and wouldn't they
feel like hell? Well, I didn't
die then, but learned to call
all we didn't comprehend
gaps in understanding, becoming,
as those with fortune do, more
of who I was. No one is more
than one sheet thrown to the wind,
folded and refolded, becoming what
the person beside her might never
believe possible. The man from Saipan
has a window seat, he has clouds
and a stack of boarding passes
fastened with a rubber band, like
an out-sized deck of playing cards,
evidence of all the flights he's taken
this year. It's the end of December.
Flights are different from places.
Places are different from people.
In half a million miles, he's seen
mostly the inside of planes
and terminals. He says, *I like*
being in the air, without saying
what happened on the ground, but
it must have been something, don't
you think, something makes a man

crave to be in transit, to swill
chocolate milk and vodka from a paper
cup, to count passage in hundreds
of thousands of miles, to squeeze
himself into a metal tube the way
my grandparents, tumbling into
each other at the department store
where they worked, in Pittsburgh, in
1926, tucked love letters into pneumatic
tubes from ladies' hats to men's attire.
People ought to be love
letters, we ought to get sent
at Mach speeds to someone who,
tenderly, will tear us open, will
reread us constantly and continuously,
and the man from Saipan hands me
the sea and the ship and the sea
monster ready to make everything
veer off course, and I ask him
to sign it, and he does, with
xx, the way a man who can't
write does, or like one
signaling, via shorthand—
with love.

Threshold

She stood a long
time at the door

as if wanting
to come in,

as if invisible
arrows lodged

within would
forbid it.

Birdsong

There must some-
where be a forest

that's lost its
voice, which goes

deeper and deeper
into itself, its

trees never
seen again.

Hard

We wear hard
hats at all times—

even manna
has consequences.

Cloud Study

How do clouds
learn to be clouds?

They study what
Constable—seeing them—

saw: awe for sure,
but also a falling

away from any sense
of earthly surface. Zero

horizon. *Skying,* he called
his hundred sketches. Think

of the Great Wallendas stretching
netless above gorges: a cloud

learns not to look down.

Cleaving

It holds
the leaving

inside it—as
I held you—

flesh and *oh's*
in an ocean

of going.

Prayer

Dear God, give
me the strength—

in the presence
of deaf gods—

to stop praying.

Light

It looked like something
you could pick up, that

dagger of light.
He left it there,

not trusting what
he might do with it.

Tip

Always, on the tip
of his tongue, something

cold and deeply unthinkable.
Around him you

always felt sinkable.

Wedding Dress

Look closer:
she sewed it

from a hundred
tattered flags

of surrender.

Sunset

That was a red
flag and all

I could do
was run to it.

Futile

To pound at a door
that isn't there—

with her I
hounded air.

Boy in Fins

He has to walk
backwards into the sea,

as if saying goodbye
to the cliffs, to the cliff-

side shacks, to the women
knitting in lamplight

inside them. He walks back-
wards on his awkward

fins, at dusk, as if
becoming another

creature—which,
leaving all we

know, we must.

Music Class

Kids learned to play
recorder in fourth grade,

but I arrived late that year,
and Mr. Bradley, fatigued

and harried, taught me
to fake it: how to inflate

my cheeks and make
fingers navigate in the baroque

way favored for pastoral
scenes, for amorous and other

miraculous events. At frigid
Christmas concerts, I

was convincing, shivering
on bleachers, shamming

Ave Maria. Who the hell
plays a wooden flute these

days? But mastering
silence—no one forgets.

Painting the Soldiers

I ran out of blue
paint, then gray.

The lady at the paint
store gave me tubes

of orange, free of charge,
so both my cavalries,

my two bugle boys,
my generals and all my

enlisted men, step
lively, impossibly, together—

in defense of one lustrous sun.

All You Can Do

Who can keep pace
with each new dictator?

You wake up and streets
have new names.

All you can do
is stay up all night

with a girl who gets
between you and the all-

night lights of the sullen,
conscripted, all-night sign painters.

Blizzard

All night plows plow.
Snows snow. Lovers

somewhere somehow love.
What purity: doing what

you are. I listen to the bone
soup brewing: not the proper

way to savor the savory.
Let's study weather

weathering, balloons
ballooning. The weather

balloon sent up says
which way winds

howl & how fast. I'm
trying to put my mouth

around the idea of
you. It's an awkward

task—like the dog
bringing slippers

to his legless master.

How Sound Travels

You said goodbye and I
heard *good* and *I*, and

only later, the buzzing
b, its lethal sting.

Nightshade

It trades in
poison and

in balms. We
call it bitter-

sweet—what
living isn't?

II

Happiness

Happiness
is a dactyl.
It comes
from the Greek
stem meaning
finger. We come
from the Greek
diner, meaning,
with three
fingers held
aloft, to call
a cab. One
doesn't come.
Happiness
is a heaviness
carried by two
lighter beats.
We carried
the whole
snowy way
each other.

Field Trip

Today we are going
everywhere in our heads.
To go you must show
your underbelly and a note
from your mother. You
must, on your person (in
your head), carry the
following: everything.
This should include but
not be limited to: fire,
earth, air, water, snacks
for everyone and whatever
fundamental elements have
yet to be discovered.
Choose a buddy. Choose
from flora or fauna, from
window or door. Choose
wisely: orderly behavior
will not be tolerated.
Remember, you who
resemble a yellow
school bus: you are
not a representative
of the sun. You
are the sun.

Gift Economy

I give you a gift card for a store that doesn't accept gift cards.

The store is in another galaxy.

I give you a paper airplane and a paper ticket for the plane.

I let you fly the plane.

I give you the manifest, which says this is a cargo plane filled with horses.

I tell you the horses don't think of themselves as cargo.

I give you sugar cubes for the horses, and apples.

They're gifts you can look at in the horses' mouths.

I give you a flight plan and a lighter with which to ignite it.

You give me the flash fire that begs an encore.

I give you me going up in smoke.

Ajar

The day's not gone, nor
all its sweets. In windows

and in doors ajar: our
beginnings. We name

the animals and wind
Summer and *Light*—

all night they come in.

Attention Checkout

Before the exit door at the hardware
store, there's a bell you can ring if
you get excellent service, as I did
from Debbie, who went above and be-
yond, climbing an orange ladder to find
three right-sized alabaster blinds for my
bedroom. Debbie comes from Raleigh,
North Carolina, which I know because
her drawl says: *Ask me anything.* I
could have asked if she installed
blinds or blindfolds, if she could show
me the dark I've been missing.
Instead, I ring the bell and head
to the key cutting station because I
mean to read up on key parties,
and then Amy calls from Iowa:
You should move back here, she says.
I've got prospects for you. I've got
a paper sack that says: *Attention
checkout, beware of shoplifters.* I
pocket the keys and give the checkout
clerk my blinds and five citrus air
fresheners that take me back, not
to Iowa City in '83, but to Miami,
in '75, when I was a kid and got
lost in an orange grove and discovered
happiness. It's what the astronauts

drink: the idea of someone counting
down to your return. That
happiness didn't last. Someone
found me and I got grounded, which
is the last thing an astronaut wants.
Linda craves frankness. Alexa says
she could use a man in a uniform
of the losing army. I listen to what
people want even if I can't
give it to them, which may or
may not constitute excellent service.
Linda has excellent lips with which
someone else will get to experiment.
Alexa has a husband who builds
bridges to invisible cities. I
have a decision to make: pay
for the keys or steal them. Linda
compares herself to Stiva in *Anna Karenina*,
because she's never hurt anyone
too much for too long. The human body
contains trace amounts of zinc and iron
and copper and I could give her the key
to my city, and she could melt it down
for a bell to ring for someone I'll
never meet, and my wretchedness
would be like no one else's.

Summer, Lake

You can't fish
for light, or

you can, but
you have to

throw it back.

Midcentury

after Ritsos

Others had houses
with floors. He

had a door,
which was an awkward

thing to carry, and
heavy—yet he never

tired of saying
to anyone on his

only road: *Come in.*

Thousands Flee

They bring their
anguish with them.
They've torn an opening
in the chain-link fence,
they're at the border
of nothing and nothing and
someone's clutching what
at such an awkward angle
should be a doll, but isn't.
A pacifier hangs
from its neck.
The fence is not
a miracle that parts
on their behalf,
and the boats they load
themselves onto we
won't call ships, nor sea-
worthy, and who among
us, vessels in distress,
circling and sinking, is
worthy of this earth?

Declarative

I give you
broken

things, so
you won't

ask: *Will
this break?*

To the Sun

Come back
so I
can forgive you.

In Finland

In a certain Finnish village by a lake,
on a certain lane, by a certain thorn-

hemmed door, it's poor form to knock
just once. I'm certain this is so, and why

at every door marked *Fin*
I knock once more.

Stationery

In the stationery store, he asks
for the sort of pencil that's mostly

eraser. What do you call that?
he asks, and the clerk isn't sure

whether he means what do you
call that sort of pencil or what

do you call the desire for it.
But she understands what's

behind the question, and behind
her counter there's a room where

quietly, they erase each other.

Fontainebleau

We're in the library, high
as the kites that kites

fly, eyeing the massive globe
on which Napoleon lay

his hand, imagining
all the lands that would

be his. How that world
must have spun

to escape him. In
the winter gardens,

we lunch on blood
oranges. A train comes,

and one gray cloud. I
will forsake you.

Crossing

He walks like a condemned man,
putting one sprig of green

in front of a blizzard.
Mostly he travels by night,

in dreams, to not be seen.
By day he hangs out

with other condemned men—
they eat, they laugh, play cards.

Tomorrow they will tell
their condemned women

how the hours, like yellow
tulips to light, bend toward them.

Portrait

Cézanne tells his friend
to sit like an apple,

and there she is—
fallen for all of eternity.

Omitting Beauty and Green

after Hikmet

My hands advance, the light
is hungry, a road through

my eyes runs. The world must
somewhere be blooming

enough. I like being
inside mulberries, captured.

The point is the window.
The sunny infirmary

can't smell the carnations.
Beside hopeful trees, the prison

                                             surrenders.

After Horace

The dark boat that bears
us away—tell me

that's the one, coming
here, that sank.

Early Fervor

I came across a small
book of prayer. I

was a big child.
It was like trying

to ride the wrong-
sized icicle.

Street Corner

He asked me to hold
something. I think

what I held
was his believing

he'd be back.

Shadow Of

The shadow my mother
makes she makes

by mistake. *Take
two*, she says, rearranging

us in front of the camera,
in front of the brick

wall that is the sea we
are forbidden to drown

or swim in. All these
years we stare her

down, sullen, sun-
blinded. What was

the photo meant
to document? Not

that we were there—
or anywhere—but that

someone was looking.

Before and After

The horse came
before the cart.

The cart came
after we had

places that no
longer loved us.

Far came
before farther.

And the whips,
and the distance—

which came first?

Second Seder

My father forgets where
light bulbs go, how long

a three-minute egg
should cook, or to mention

he's got a new wife.
She moved in with her own

ghosts. She isn't evil and
remembers not to wear

many of my mother's dresses.
At Passover she finds

a shank bone and roasts
it, she finds the awkward

bowl I made my mother
(clay—the bowl, my mother)

when I was ten. My mother
kept gumdrops, bedside, in it.

The second wife fills it with salt
water. My people are always

leaving: any vessel, for dipping
bitter herbs, suffices.

Sweater

It comes with an extra
button stitched into

the inside seam: no
idea of warmth

is complete without
the promise of what

must unravel.

Salad Days

The cab I was
in passed too
fast for me
to say whether
that place we
loved was renamed
the Fatted or
the Fated Calf.
Names change,
and appetites,
and things
end badly
for the calf
either way,
though every-
thing in the rear
view seems green.

To the Woman Going Up the Escalator at Columbus Circle at Five-Thirty Last Evening

You were holding
a fortunate orchid.
I was not
the slob standing
beside you. I
was the slob behind,
one who'd live
happily on half
an ice cube
now and again
to ascend once
to a blue
moon with you.

III

Night

Someone was talking
quietly of lanterns—

but loud enough
to light my way.

Establishing Shot

The entry
wound by

which I
knew you.

Harvest

The pears I did
not give you six

years back can't
stop rotting.

Underfoot

Where the hound
lounged, now

his shadow. One
stumbles.

Skin in Game

It isn't easy giving
your skin to someone

to hold, even for
a minute, even if she

gives you her skin, or
the bones of her inner

ear without blinking.
You can't hear

without those bones,
you need someone

to intuit winds
closing in. Without

skin you feel too
much this buffeting,

the way grasses,
flaming, die back,

the way a solitary
mare through green

fields moves,
the way the field

moves through you.

On Divinity

I believe in divine
intervention. When

the gods rush past,
I tackle them.

Knitted Owl

The knitted owl begins
with a knitted brow—
not the owl's, but yours,
contorted, browsing patterns.
Anything can be knitted.
The trick is making
a decision, which is a kind
of incision. In the decision to knit
the owl is the decision not
to knit everything else, at least
not this minute. Decisions get
knitted together, with needles,
in lamb's wool, in a cast-
on stitch. The owl you knit
has wings from one pattern,
torso from another, because flight
isn't the point here: this owl
will be a pillow the pink of a weeping
cherry in which an actual
owl might roost. You give it
rum-colored buttons for eyes.
You pour yourself a tumbler
of sun in a sage green room.
It's a forest in which you recall
conflicting myths about owls:
how wise they are, how
foolish, how feared, how

admired, how we make
the night describe
everything inside us.

The Way Forward

Swordplay is all
the rage at Edie's
school. You can't have
an actual sword but
may display the swagger
of your arm, which Rupert
does, all blade and swashbuckle,
though he must ask Edie
first, *May I wave my saber
at you?* Or, drawing the two
fingers of his pistol, *May
I shoot?* Edie rolls
her eyes—*Yes, yes,* lets
Rupert pull the trigger,
then spins, then topples, then
plays dead. She's expert
at that, and when Rupert
moves toward her, searching
for a pulse, faint breath, for a way
to take it all back, there's no
one to ask permission of,
no one to say that the way
he goes now isn't the gang-
plank of his making.

Experimental

He builds the birds
from wings he has

around the house,
the cage from bread

he bakes. He means
to see how long the birds

might take to eat
a way out, how long,

not knowing the ways
of the wild, to fly

back, and in what
forlorn and minor

key, for their stale
cage, sing.

Winter

The moths have sewn
another hole
into my sweater.

Exile

She writes from an island
with too much wind.

There's enough to lift
the green from palms,

enough to grip her
doomed sarong,

enough to fill
sails of the boat

desire builds.

The New World

See something—
slay something!

More Stones

for Philip Levine

Donald Justice has died twice:
once in Miami, in the sun, on a Sunday,
and once in Iowa City, on a Friday
in August, which was not without
its own sun—if not bright spot.
The first time he died, he was thinking
of Vallejo, who died in Paris, maybe
on a Thursday, surely in rain.
Vallejo died again in Paris,
in April, of an unknown illness
which may have been malaria,
as fictionalized in Bolaño's
Monsieur Pain. "There is, brothers,
very much to do," Vallejo said
between his deaths, and Phil,
you must have died once
in Seville, in the land of Machado,
before going again last Saturday
in Fresno, so you no longer write
to us or bring in trash bins filled
with light. Phil, I will die, maybe
on a Sunday in Wellfleet, because
today it is Sunday, and ice
is jamming the eaves, and there
is nowhere to put the snow

that keeps recalling all
those other snows—
or the stones
on more stones.

Just

Just
imagining

the branch
as gallows

makes it
break.

Catalogue Of

What isn't
perishable
isn't.

Worry

Will there be
enough beads?

Another Blizzard

The snow is in
the other room—
don't go in there.

Yarn

How many skeins
she left, and patterns

neatly creased, and
needles, and rebellious, I

never learned to knit.
I was learning to be cold.

Long Haul

He wants to go
back to a place

that never was. I
will go with him.

Fellow Traveler

She went everywhere
with an empty suitcase.

You never know when
you'll need to leave

swiftly with nothing.

Carrots & Sticks

In a pinch, a carrot
can double as a stick—

but the stick, no
matter how hard

you hit it, persists
as a switch from which

even the dumbest
bunny in chuffed

fluffles runs.

Light Show

It's not the birds
that are flying
away   no   it is
the trees   not
me saying hang
around but the river
that brought you
here   it is
the golden light
on the tray of late
summer   it is late
autumn we are in
the thicket of it early
yet in the lives
of minerals   of glaciers
the hours are
calving the clocks
listening in   we
should hurry and show
the light what
we mean to make of it

Smoke Signals

All of the
above

but not
for long.

All Night

The driving
rain—where
will it take us?

Acknowledgments

I am grateful to the editors of these journals, in which the following poems appeared, sometimes in slightly different incarnations.

Agni Online: "Establishing Shot," "Smoke Signals"; *American Academy of Poetry:* "More Stones"; *Arkansas International:* "Prayer," "To the Woman Going Up the Escalator at Columbus Circle at Five-Thirty Last Evening"; *Berfrois:* "The New World"; *Cincinnati Review:* "Futile," "Tip," "Happiness"; *cream city review:* "Before and After," "Spell"; *Diode:* "Cleaving," "Gift Economy," "Stationery," "Winter"; *ELKE:* "Threshold"; *Fitchburg Sentinel and Enterprise Alphabet Project:* "Ajar," "Thousands Flee"; *Gli Stati Generali:* "Midcentury"; *Great River Review:* "After Horace," "Boy in Fins"; *Harvard Divinity Bulletin:* "Division Of"; *Incessant Pipe:* "All You Can Do"; *JuxtaProse:* "Harvest," "Salad Days"; *Kenyon Review:* "Nightshade"; *The Literary Review:* "Attention Checkout," "Action Origami," "Early Fervor," "Yarn"; *Memorious:* "Painting the Soldiers," "Shadow Of"; *The New Yorker:* "Major to Minor," "Cloud Study"; *Plume:* "Fountainebleau," "The Way Forward," "Knitted Owl," "Nights With"; *Post Road:* "The Size of It"; *Poetry Daily:* "Happiness"; *Soundings:* "Sweater"; *The Tablet:* "Second Seder"; *Terrain:* "Birdsong," "Night," "Just," "Light," "Fellow Traveler," "Skin in Game," "Street Corner," "Summer, Lake," "Crossing," "Experimental," "Blizzard"; *Tikkun:* "Omitting Beauty and Green"; *Tin House:* "Declarative," "Field Trip," "To the Sun"; and *upstreet:* "Light Show."

A balm, all: Francesca Bewer, Olga Broumas, Gail Caldwell, Sarah Harwell, Danielle Jones, Miriam Kahn, Sarah Keniston, Gail Mazur, Jane Mead, Kiel Moe, Lise Motherwell, Giavanna Munafo, Carl Safina, Alice Sebold, Andy Senchak, Tom Sleigh, Bob Steinberg, Jean Wilcox, and my brothers. Deep thanks to the MacDowell Colony and to Martha Rhodes and everyone at Four Way. And Naomi Wallace (ideal reader), you still rock.

Andrea Cohen's poems have appeared in *The New Yorker, Atlantic Monthly, Poetry, The Threepenny Review, The New Republic,* and elsewhere. Her earlier poetry collections include *Unfathoming, Furs Not Mine, Kentucky Derby, Long Division,* and *The Cartographer's Vacation.* She directs the Blacksmith House Poetry Series in Cambridge, MA and the Writers House at Merrimack College.

Publication of this book was made possible by grants and donations. We are also grateful to those individuals who participated in our 2018 Build a Book Program. They are:

Anonymous (11), Vincent Bell, Jan Bender-Zanoni, Laurel Blossom, Adam Bohanon, Lee Briccetti, Jane Martha Brox, Carla & Steven Carlson, Andrea Cohen, Janet S. Crossen, Marjorie Deninger, Patrick Donnelly, Charles Douthat, Blas Falconer, Monica Ferrell, Joan Fishbein, Jennifer Franklin, Sarah Freligh, Helen Fremont & Donna Thagard, Robert Fuentes & Martha Webster, Ryan George, Panio Gianopoulos, Lauri Grossman, Julia Guez, Naomi Guttman & Jonathan Mead, Steven Haas, Bill & Cam Hardy, Lori Hauser, Ricardo Hernandez, Bill Holgate, Deming Holleran, Piotr Holysz, Nathaniel Hutner, Rebecca Kaiser Gibson, Voki Kalfayan, David Lee, Sandra Levine, Howard Levy, Owen Lewis, Jennifer Litt, Sara London & Dean Albarelli, David Long, Ralph & Mary Ann Lowen, Jacquelyn Malone, Fred Marchant, Louise Mathias, Catherine McArthur, Nathan McClain, Richard McCormick, Kamilah Aisha Moon, Beth Morris, Rebecca & Daniel Okrent, Jill Pearlman, Marcia & Chris Pelletiere, Maya Pindyck, Megan Pinto, Eileen Pollack, Barbara Preminger, Kevin Prufer, Martha Rhodes, Paula Rhodes, Linda Safyan, Peter & Jill Schireson, Jason Schneiderman, Roni & Richard Schotter, Jane Scovel, Andrew Seligsohn & Martina Anderson, Soraya Shalforoosh, Julie A. Sheehan, James Snyder & Krista Fragos, Alice St. Claire-Long, Megan Staffel, Dorothy Tapper Goldman, Marjorie & Lew Tesser, Boris Thomas, Connie Voisine, Calvin Wei, Bill Wenthe, Allison Benis White, Michelle Whittaker, Rachel Wolff, and Anton Yakovlev.